Journeys with Jesus

JESUS, MY ROCK—HE ROCKS

RITA HUTCHINGS

Inspiring Voices books may be ordered through booksellers or by contacting:

Inspiring Voices
1663 Liberty Drive
Bloomington, IN 47403
www.inspiringvoices.com
1-(866) 697-5313

Because of the dynamic nature of the Internet, any web addresses or links contained in this book may have changed since publication and may no longer be valid. The views expressed in this work are solely those of the author and do not necessarily reflect the views of the publisher, and the publisher hereby disclaims any responsibility for them.

Any people depicted in stock imagery provided by Thinkstock are models, and such images are being used for illustrative purposes only. Certain stock imagery © Thinkstock.

ISBN: 978-1-4624-0819-1 (sc)
ISBN: 978-1-4624-0820-7 (e)

Printed in the United States of America.

Inspiring Voices rev. date: 4/30/2014

Scripture taken from the Holy Bible, NEW INTERNATIONAL VERSION®. Copyright © 1973, 1978, 1984 by Biblica, Inc. All rights reserved worldwide. Used by permission. NEW INTERNATIONAL VERSION® and NIV® are registered trademarks of Biblica, Inc. Use of either trademark for the offering of goods or services requires the prior written consent of Biblica US, Inc.

Scripture taken from the King James Version of the Bible.

Dedication

To those who have shared in the vision of this book with prayers and insights; it is with heartfelt gratitude to them. To Jesus. 1st and foremost, my daughter Amy, son Andy, and other family members. Friends, Patty, Monica, Dorothy, Paula, Dolores and Art. May the blessings of these messages within these pages, be given to them, and for all those who desire for God to blaze a new trail in their hearts like never before.

Preface

The growth, and His love, imparted in this book comes from what He is doing in my garden of the heart. He continues to change my life. He wants me to share it in this way. It is my prayer that what is expressed herein, is touched by His hand, as He speaks to your hearts.

Acknowledgment

To those who shared this vision of The Journey with Jesus having insights and support. Thank you for believing in one, for this finished work of God's Garden in us, Paula, Janelle, Rosemary, Jordan, and many others including Inspiring Voices Staff, who have been cheering me on right from the beginning.

It is right, that a special dedication for Karina, my seven year old granddaughter, for her contribution of a flower and a bee is included. Just as He watches them, He watches us. Karina is a special little girl who loves God, and her picture is a welcome addition to this theme.

A tribute to Don Hutchings is fitting also at this time. Amy and Andy, my daughter and son, along with me and my granddaughter Karina, want to pay respects to his memory.

Don has passed away several years ago now. He is known to be with Jesus and that is our comfort. We think of him often, with love. He never knew Karina on this earth, but it is known he sees her now and all he cared for while he was here. We have a lot of fond memories of him. He is remembered as one who enjoyed life and with God's help, overcame many obstacles along the way. There came a time in his life when he opened his heart to Jesus and God's forgiveness flooded within him. He spent enjoyable times with his children, with family and friends. He partook of community service minded activities. Don was fun loving and outgoing but he also had grief and sorrow. He released himself to God during an illness and let God take over. Don was so glad to do so, and a total heart change occurred.

Thought of Don crept in while this book was coming together. *Included are some of the places that he knew. While Don lived life here, he lived with an intense flair all his own. This book comes from the hand of God. What Don had shared with those who love him, we remember. In this, he shares a portion of these pages.*

A special acknowledgment to Ron B., who was instrumental in leading Don to our Savior, Jesus. Words aren't always enough to express it to you Ron, but thank you from our hearts to you for your obedience to God.

Expansions of Don's and my family tree are, Andy, Amy and Karina. They are the new
flowers that have been rooted in our garden. They are taking in, where God has planted
them, more and more of the soil surrounding them. The richness of His nutrients
of Grace are there. This is ensuring future growth in the best possible way.

NIV Matt 6:25-28

So I tell you to stop worrying about what you eat, drink and wear. Isn't life more than clothes? Behold the birds of the air, for they do not sow, neither do they reap, nor gather into barns; Your heavenly Father feeds them. Are you not much more valuable than they? Which of you can add even one inch to his stature? Take no thought for clothing. Watch the lilies of the field, how they grow; they don't toil, and they don't spin.

NIV Matt 6:31-34

When you seek the Kingdom of God first, and all of His righteousness, all of these things will be added to you. Take no thought for these things, therefore, for tomorrow will take care of itself.

NIV 1 Chronicles 16:27

Splendor and majesty go before Him; praise and joy are in His holy place.

NIV Ps 27:14

Wait for the Lord; be strong and take heart and wait for the Lord.

NIV Isaiah 58:9-11

You shall call on the Lord, and He shall say, here I am. If you do away with the pointing finger and malicious talk and if you spend yourselves in behalf of the hungry and satisfy the needs of the oppressed, then your light will rise in the darkness and your light will become like noon-day. The Lord will guide you always; He will satisfy your needs in a scorched land and will strengthen your frame. You are like a well-watered garden; like a spring whose waters never fail.

NIV Jeremiah 23:23-24

"Am I a God near at hand," says the Lord, "and not a God far off?
Can anyone hide himself in secret places, so I shall not see him?
Do I not fill heaven and earth? Says the Lord.

NIV Ps 91:1

He who dwells in the secret place of the Most High, shall abide under the shadow of the almighty

The soil of our hearts can't help but change to be more and more fertile, when we yield To Him. Our roots go deep into the words of Jesus and they become a part of us.

As seasons change, and things look different, as with a snow cover, compared with other changes, transformation happens. Even when we can't see them right away. God is up to something-something wonderful. When we pray, sometimes there is a quick manifestation. Other times, we need to keep on believing, even though we don't see it happen with our eyes like we think it should. God's timing is always better than our own, Prayers are like seeds, sent to the Father, opening up on the way to Him. These start in our hearts, and He sees that. Just as a farmer starts to see what he has planted spring forth, so it is with us. The intended result depends on how much of the word we get into us and how we respond to it as it enters our hearts.

With the right kind of nurturing in a garden, such as water, sunshine and a caring hand, healthy growth occurs. It takes also, a cool, gentle breath of God blowing over them. It's a vital part of it all. When we come with a right heart, we can come to Him; we can ask what we will in accordance with His will, and be confident that He hears us, Any good thing you see, has come about by prayer. This is awesome to think about. His gentle, life-giving breath is in and on us as well.

He is the master of all we need, and it is Him over everything. He changes hearts and lives, when we look to Him. With the Master Gardener by our sides, and with His constant care, we get grounded and rooted in Him when we choose to abide. We are more likely to be sustained when changes and storms come. We are able to withstand them, as He sees us through to the other side with victory.

God listens. Take time to listen and hear His voice. It whispers our names and says, "This is the way; follow Me."

He gives the water that springs up inside of us, called Eternal Life. Transformation in us occurs through His living water in this life, as well as into the next. As we drink in this living water, profound changes occur in us as only He can do.

KJV Ps New Testament
Ps 85:12

Yea, the Lord shall give that which is good, and the land shall yield her increase.

NIV Galatians 5:22

But the fruit of the Spirit is love, joy, peace, patience, kindness, goodness,
gentleness and self-control. Against such things there is no law.

KJV New Testament Ps
Ps 40:16

Blessed be the Lord, who loads us with benefits, the God of my salvation.

Kid's Application Bible
Isaiah 61:10-11

Let me tell you of how happy God has made me: For He clothed me with garments of salvation
and draped about me the robe of righteousness, like a bridegroom in his wedding suit or a bride
with her jewels. The Lord will show the nations of the world His justice. His righteousness shall be
as a budding tree, or like a garden in early spring, full of young plants springing up everywhere.

NIV Hosea 14:7

Men will dwell again in his shade, he will flourish like the grain. He will blossom
like the vine, and his fame will be like the wine from Lebanon.

KJV New Testament Ps
Ps 104:10

He sends the springs into the valleys, which are among the hills.

NIV Genesis 1:11

Then God said, "Let the land produce vegetation: seed bearing plants and trees on the land that bear fruit with seed in it, according to their various kinds." And it was so.

NIV Luke 21:30

When their buds burst open, you see for yourselves, and know that summer is near.

Kid's Application Bible
Ps 96:12

Praise Him for the growing fields, for they display His greatness.
Let the trees rustle in the forest, with praise,

The love of God keeps and carries us through triumphantly with whatever happens in our days, as we trust in Him.

When we are rescued from the old nature, we are taken from Satan's grip and from sin's control over us. Because Jesus walked the way of the cross for us, the crown of thorns, the beatings, scourgings, the nails and all that that means, He made a way for us to know what it is that He accomplished at the cross. To be bought back from Satan and sin and dying in those sins. All of humanity has come, and continues to come, in that state, being with the old nature. Our condition cried out for a Savior and was heard in heaven. He took on humanity to cause us to have Eternal life with Him, to be redeemed and bought back, because we couldn't do it ourselves. It had to be a perfect sacrifice. Never having to be done again. Jesus took the keys of sin and death from Satan. Therefore, we are covered by the Blood of the Lamb, Jesus. To use the Sword of the Spirit, which is the Word of God against the flesh and Satan. Jesus has given us this authority to do so. It's that power that raised Jesus from the grave, that we have when we accept Him. Now that's ultimate power: That is why He said from the cross, "It is finished."

God reveals Himself in countless ways. He loves us. His love shines through the centuries today, to us. God gave His best gift to us. His son Jesus, with what He went through at Calvary and all that that means; when we accept Him as Lord and Savior, we have the opportunity to receive the most precious gift. To be rescued from the old nature and embrace the new life He has for us in Christ Jesus.

NIV Ps 113:3

From the rising of the sun to the place where it sets, the name of the Lord is to be praised.

Even in nature, God causes seeds to grow, as they burst forth for our benefit. Grasses, flowers and crops of the fields. The giving of these things, are for our sustenance; being the blessings that they are, while we are on this earth. He gives showers, His thunders and lightnings, snow and His sunshine. All in His time. The birds of the air, and the flowers of the fields He cares for, but ever so much for us. We need to see Him in these things; sensing His loving hands, caring for His creation. Just as God's little creatures, such as the birds of the air, and animals of the fields rely on His keeping, so much more then, do we need to rely on His, for ours.

To live the life we need, is to accept His plan and live all He has for us. He is putting it into action then. These processes need to take place for our walk with Him, to be a walk that is intimate. That includes our prayer life. He knows we can't do it alone. He is with us every step of the way. In these changes we need to make, there needs to be from us, an acknowledgement we have come to know personally: For every part of our lives. Some growth starts slow, others come up more quickly. Others still, require more time. It is a commitment of growth and ultimately bearing His good fruit. Fruits of the Spirit, such as His peace, compassion and so much more to be like Him in greater quantity. The plan He has for us is one of a future and a hope. In knowing how He loves us, choose to open up the garden gate of your heart to Him and watch Him change your life.

NIV Romans 15:13

May the God of hope fill you with all joy and peace as you trust Him, so that
you may overflow with hope by the power of the Holy Spirit.

Growth in us delights Father God when we grow in His way, We are also made to delight in this progress we make from day to day. It should draw others to Him, as they observe and behold this growth, The gardener has to prepare the soil, watch for weeds, bugs, and so forth and to take the appropriate steps against them. Our heavenly Father has to do the same with us.

Flowers of the field have such a variety. Some are producing edible, succulent, nutritious blueberries and blackberries that grow for us. The outcome is always delicious. They are all yielding to His touch, and everything He has put within them for growing as they do. It takes a heart that is yielded to Him and His word. This creates in us the soil needed to experience heart changes as we should. He blesses us so much when we are willing.

Each sort of plant that grows in the field and garden; plants, herbs and flowers grow because of Him and are beneficial to us. There is something so satisfying to see all of these things growing in the field or in any other way that they do, Whether it's the gardener, others who pass by, or whoever partakes of them in any way, it speaks to the heart of their goodness.

We need to do our part in this journey with Him. Taking out the rocky, stony, thorny parts of our hearts has to occur. With hearts open to Him and to these ways of what He is doing, He is accomplishing His plans for our lives.

Sometimes, it can be painful but it is necessary that we respond to Him and to the ways He chooses to do what He needs to do in our gardens. We will receive all of His benefits and yield the harvest as we are destined to possess.

NIV John 4:14

Whoever drinks the water I give him will never thirst. Indeed, the water I give
him will become in him a spring of water welling up to eternal life.

NIV Ps 37:3

Trust in the Lord and do good and truly you will dwell in the land, and enjoy safe pasture.

NIV Ezekiel 34:26

I will save them and the places all around, My hill, a blessing and will call showers
to come down in their seasons. There shall be showers of blessings.

NIV Luke 1:53

The Lord has filled the hungry with good things.

NIV Ps 103:2

Bless the Lord, o my soul: do not forget all the gifts of God.

KJV New Testament Ps
Ps 103:5

Who satisfies my mouth with good things, so that my youth is renewed like the eagles.

Kid's Application Bible
Genesis 1:21-22

So God created great sea animals and every sort of fish and every kind of
bird. God looked at them with pleasure and blessed them all.

"Multiply and stock the oceans," He told them, and to the birds He
said, "Let your numbers increase and fill the earth."

New Testament Ps
Ps 74:17

You have set all the borders of the earth; You have made summer and winter.

NIV Genesis 8:22

While the earth remains, seedtime and harvest and heat and cold,
summer and winter and day and night will not cease.

KJV New Testament Ps 135:7

He causes the vapors to ascend from the ends of the earth; He makes the
lightnings for the rain; He brings the wind out of His treasuries.

KJV New Testament Ps
Ps 5:3

My voice shall you hear in the morning, O Lord: In the morning
will I direct my prayer unto you and will look up.

NIV Isaiah 30:23

He will also send you rain for the seeds you plant. The ground will yield the food that comes from His hand. The land will be rich and plentiful. In that day, your cattle will graze in broad meadows.

Kid's Application Bible
Isaiah 55:12

You will live in joy and peace. The mountains and hills, the trees
of the field-all the world around you shall rejoice.

KJV New Testament Ps
Ephes 1:19

And what is the exceeding power of greatness to us who believe;
according to His putting forth His great power.

NIV Prov 25:25

As cold waters to a thirsty soul, so is good news from a far country.

NIV Prov 18:4

The words of a man's mouth are as deep waters, and the wellspring of wisdom as a flowing brook.

KJV New Testament Ps
Ps 107:35

He turns the wilderness into a standing water; and dry ground into water springs.

KJV New Testament Ps
Ps 104:31

The glory of the Lord shall endure forever; the Lord shall rejoice in His works.

NIV Prov 11:30

The fruit of the righteous is a tree of life; and he that wins souls is wise.

KJV New Testament Ps
Ps 62:1-2

Truly my soul waits upon God; from Him comes my salvation.

KJV New Testament Ps
Ps 62:6

He only is my rock and my salvation; He is my defense; I shall not be greatly moved.

KJV New Testament Ps
Ps 147:8

He who covers the heaven with clouds, who prepares rain for the
earth, who makes grass to grow upon the mountains.

NIV Job 35:5

Look up to the skies and behold, regard the heavens above you.

KJV New Testament Ps
Ps 95:1

O come, let us sing unto the Lord, let us make a joyful noise to the rock of our salvation.

KJV New Testament Ps
Ps 19:1

The heavens declare the glory of God; and the firmament shows His handiwork.

KJV New Testament Ps
Ps 108:4

For your mercy is great above the heavens; and your truth reaches into the clouds.

NIV Ps 29:4

The voice of the Lord is mighty. The voice of the Lord is majestic.

KJV New Testament Ps
Ps 8:1

O Lord, our Lord, how excellent is your name in all the earth. Who has set your glory above the heavens.

NIV Ps 147:16

He gives snow like wool; He scatters the hoarfrost like ashes.

KJV New Testament Ps
Ps 97:4

His lightnings enlightened the world: The earth saw and trembled.

NIV Heb 1:14

Are not all angels ministering spirits sent to serve them who will inherit salvation?

Kid's Application Bible
John 1:51

You will even see heaven open and the angels of God coming back and forth to Me, the Messiah.

KJV New Testament Ps
Acts 14:22

We must, through tribulation, enter the Kingdom of God.

Printed in the United States
By Bookmasters